TO

_____

FROM

_____

HOW TO FIND

HOPE

The quoted ideas expressed in this book (but not scripture verses) are not, in all cases, exact quotations, as some have been edited for clarity and brevity. In all cases, the author has attempted to maintain the speaker's original intent. In some cases, quoted material for this book was obtained from secondary sources, primarily print media. While every effort was made to ensure the accuracy of these sources, the accuracy cannot be guaranteed. For additions, deletions, corrections or clarifications in future editions of this text, please write BRIGHTON BOOKS.

Scripture quotations are taken from:

The Holy Bible, King James Version

The Holy Bible, New International Version (NIV) Copyright © 1973, 1978, 1984, by International Bible Society. Used by permission of Zondervan Publishing House. All rights reserved.

The Holy Bible, New King James Version (NKJV) Copyright © 1982 by Thomas Nelson, Inc. Used by permission.

The New American Standard Bible®, (NASB) Copyright © 1960, 1962, 1963, 1968, 1971, 1972, 1973, 1975, 1977, 1995 by The Lockman Foundation. Used by permission.

New Century Version®. (NCV) Copyright © 1987, 1988, 1991 by Word Publishing, a division of Thomas Nelson, Inc. All rights reserved. Used by permission.

The Holman Christian Standard Bible™ (HCSB) Copyright © 1999, 2000, 2001 by Holman Bible Publishers. Used by permission.

Cover Design by Kim Russell / Wahoo Designs
Page Layout by Bart Dawson

ISBN 1-58334-214-1

Printed in the United States of America

TABLE OF CONTENTS

INTRODUCTION

Everywhere we turn, or so it seems, we are confronted with an ever-growing collection of "how-to" books. Many of these books are helpful, but none can compare with the ultimate how-to guide: God's Holy Word. The Bible is a book unlike any other. It is a guidebook for life on earth and for life eternal. It contains the seeds of hope and the promise of salvation. This text is intended to assist you as you consider God's Word and meditate upon its meaning for your life.

Perhaps you have encountered situations that have left you discouraged, disheartened, or worse. Perhaps the suffering of today has robbed you of hope for tomorrow. Perhaps you are enduring unwelcome changes or life-altering losses. If so, each chapter in this book should serve as a powerful reminder that God still sits in His heaven and that His promises still apply *to you*. Don't think for a moment that God is a distant, disinterested observer. He is, instead, an ever-present partner in every aspect of your life.

This text contains 30 devotional readings that can lift your spirits, lower your anxieties, and raise your hopes. As you contemplate your own circumstances, remember this: whatever the size of your problems, God is bigger. Much bigger. He will instruct you, protect you, energize you, and heal you . . . *if* you let Him. So pray fervently, listen carefully, work diligently, and hope mightily. Do your best and trust God with the rest. Then, you can rest assured: whatever "it" is, God can handle it . . . and will.

WHERE HOPE BEGINS

I will lift up my eyes to the hills—From whence comes my help? My help comes from the LORD, Who made heaven and earth.

Psalm 121:1-2 NKJV

The hope that the world offers is fleeting and imperfect. The hope that God offers is unchanging, unshakable, and unending. It is no wonder, then, that when we seek security from worldly sources, our hopes are often dashed. Thankfully, God has no such record of failure.

Where will you place your hopes today? Will you entrust your future to man or to God? Will you seek solace exclusively from fallible human beings, or will you place your hopes, first and foremost, in the trusting hands of your Creator? The decision is yours, and you must live with the results of the choice you make.

For thoughtful believers, hope begins with God. Period. So today, as you embark upon the next stage of your life's journey, consider the words of the psalmist: "You are my hope; O Lord GOD, You are my confidence" (71:5 NASB). Then, place your trust in the One who cannot be shaken.

And because we know Christ is alive, we have hope for the present and hope for life beyond the grave.

Billy Graham

Faith looks back and draws courage; hope looks ahead and keeps desire alive.

John Eldredge

Love is the seed of all hope. It is the enticement to trust, to risk, to try, and to go on.

Gloria Gaither

Hope is nothing more than the expectation of those things which faith has believed to be truly promised by God.

John Calvin

Happy is he…whose hope is in the LORD his God.
Psalm 146:5 KJV

∞ PRAYER

Dear Lord, let my hopes begin and end with you. When I am discouraged, let me turn to You. When I am weak, let me find strength in You. You are my Father, and I will place my faith, my trust, and my hopes in You, this day and forever. Amen

∞ MORE VERSES TO CONSIDER

Hebrews 10:23
Lamentations 3:25-26
Psalm 119:116
Psalm 38:15

TRUSTING
THE FATHER

Trust the LORD your God with all your heart
and lean not on your own understanding;
in all your ways acknowledge him,
and he will make your paths straight.

Proverbs 3:5-6 NIV

If we believe in God, we should trust in God. Yet sometimes, when we are besieged by fears and doubts, trusting God is hard indeed.

Trusting God means trusting Him with every aspect of our lives. We must trust Him with our relationships and our finances. We must follow His commandments and pray for His guidance. When we experience the inevitable pains of life here on earth, we must accept God's will and seek His healing touch. And at times, we must be willing to wait patiently for God to reveal plans that only He can see.

Are you willing to trust God completely, or are you still sitting squarely on the spiritual fence? The answer to this question will determine the tone, the quality, and the direction of your life.

When you trust your heavenly Father without reservation, you can be sure that, in His own fashion and in His own time, God will bless you in ways that you never could have imagined. So trust Him. And then prepare yourself for the abundance and the joy that will most certainly be yours when you do.

To know God as He really is—in His essential nature and character—is to arrive at a citadel of peace that circumstances may storm but can never capture.

Catherine Marshall

God is God. He knows what He is doing. When you can't trace His hand, trust His heart.

Max Lucado

Trusting God doesn't change our circumstances. Perfect trust in Him changes us.

Charles Swindoll

True faith is man's weakness leaning on God's strength.

D. L. Moody

And he said: "The LORD is my rock and my fortress and my deliverer; the God of my strength, in whom I will trust."

2 Samuel 22:2-3 NKJV

∞ PRAYER

Lord, when I trust in the things of this earth, I will be disappointed. But, when I put my faith in You, I am secure. In every aspect of my life, Lord, let me trust in Your boundless grace . . . today, tomorrow, and forever. Amen

∞ MORE VERSES TO CONSIDER

Psalm 31:1
Psalm 32:10
1 Chronicles 5:20
Proverbs 16:20

BEYOND WORRY

*This is why I tell you: Don't worry about your life,
what you will eat or what you will drink; or about
your body, what you will wear. Isn't life more than food
and the body more than clothing? Look at the birds of
the sky: they don't sow or reap or gather into barns,
yet your heavenly Father feeds them. Aren't you worth
more than they?*

Matthew 6:25-26 HCSB

Because we have the ability to think, we also have the ability to worry. All of us, even the most faithful believers, are plagued by occasional periods of discouragement and doubt. Even though we hold tightly to God's promise of salvation— even though we believe sincerely in God's love and protection—we may find ourselves fretting over the countless details of everyday life.

Because of His humanity, Jesus understood the inevitability of worry. And He addressed the topic clearly and forcefully in the sixth chapter of Matthew:

Therefore I say to you, do not worry about your life, what you will eat or what you will drink; nor about your body, what you will put on. Is not life more than food and the body more than clothing? Look at the birds of the air, for they neither sow nor reap nor gather into barns; yet your heavenly Father feeds them. Are you not of more value than they? Which of you by worrying can add one cubit to his stature? . . . Therefore do not worry about tomorrow, for tomorrow will worry about its own things. Sufficient for the day is its own trouble. vv. 25-27, 34 NKJV

Perhaps you feel disturbed by the past or threatened by the future. Perhaps you are concerned about your relationships, your health, or your finances. Or perhaps you are simply a "worrier" by nature. If so, let Jesus' words serve as a reminder that today has enough worries of its own without the added weight of yesterday's regrets or tomorrow's fears. Then, perhaps, you will worry less and trust God more. And that's as it should be because God is trustworthy . . . and you are protected.

The more you meditate on God's Word, the less you will have to worry about.

Rick Warren

The secret of Christian quietness is not indifference but the knowledge that God is my Father, He loves me, and that I shall never think of anything that He will forget. Then, worry becomes an impossibility.

Oswald Chambers

Submit each day to God, knowing that He is God over all your tomorrows.

Kay Arthur

Give your cares to Him who cares for the flowers of the field. Rest assured He will also care for you.

C. H. Spurgeon

*Be anxious for nothing, but in everything by prayer
and supplication, with thanksgiving, let your requests
be made known to God.*
Philippians 4:6 NKJV

∞ PRAYER

Lord, You sent Your Son to live as a man on this earth, and You know what it means to be completely human. You understand my worries and my fears, Lord, and You forgive me when I am weak. When my faith begins to wane, help me, Lord, to trust You more. Then, with Your Holy Word on my lips and with the love of Your Son in my heart, let me live courageously, faithfully, prayerfully, and thankfully today and every day. Amen

∞ MORE VERSES TO CONSIDER

John 14:27
Philippians 4:6
Psalm 23:4
Psalm 62:8 ✓

THE POWER OF PRAYER

Be joyful in hope, patient in affliction, faithful in prayer.
Romans 12:12 NIV

"The power of prayer": these words are so familiar, yet sometimes we forget what they mean. Prayer is a powerful tool for communicating with our Creator; it is an opportunity to commune with the Giver of all things good. Prayer helps us find strength for today and hope for the future. Prayer is not a thing to be taken lightly or to be used infrequently.

Is prayer an integral part of your daily life, or is it a hit-or-miss habit? Do you "pray without ceasing," or is your prayer life an afterthought? Do you regularly pray in the solitude of the early morning darkness, or do you bow your head only when others are watching?

The quality of your spiritual life will be in direct proportion to the quality of your prayer life. Prayer changes things, and it changes you. Today, instead of turning things over in your mind, turn them over to God in prayer. Instead of worrying about your next decision, ask God to lead the way. Don't limit your prayers to meals or to bedtime. Pray constantly about things great and small. God is listening, and He wants to hear from you now.

He who kneels most stands best.

D. L. Moody

Only God can move mountains, but faith and prayer can move God.

E. M. Bounds

Our confidence in prayer comes not from who we are but from who He is. Nothing we could ask of Him could ever compare with the price He paid for us at the cross.

Henry Blackaby

When any needy heart begins to truly pray, heaven itself stirs in response.

Jim Cymbala

The intense prayer of the righteous is very powerful.
James 5:16 HCSB

∽ PRAYER

Lord, I pray to You because You desire it and because I need it. Prayer not only changes things; it also changes me. Help me, Lord, never to face the demands of the day without first spending time with You, and help me to make prayer a part of everything that I do and everything that I am. Amen

∽ MORE VERSES TO CONSIDER

2 Chronicles 7:14
Joel 2:32
Matthew 7:7-8
Matthew 21:22

EXPECTING A MIRACLE

You are the God who performs miracles;
you display your power among the peoples.
Psalm 77:14 NIV

Sometimes, because we are imperfect human beings with limited understanding and limited faith, we place limitations on God. But, God's power has no limitations. God will work miracles in our lives *if* we trust Him with everything we have and everything we are. When we do, we experience the miraculous results of His endless love and His awesome power.

Miracles, both great and small, are an integral part of everyday life, but usually, we are too busy or too cynical to notice God's handiwork. We don't expect to see miracles, so we simply overlook them.

Do you lack the faith that God can work miracles in your own life? If so, it's time to reconsider. If you have allowed yourself to become a "doubting Thomas," you are attempting to place limitations on a God who has none. Instead of doubting your heavenly Father, you must trust Him. Then, you must wait and watch . . . because something miraculous is going to happen *to you*, and it might just happen today.

We have a God who delights in impossibilities.

Andrew Murray

Faith means believing in realities that go beyond sense and sight. It is the awareness of unseen divine realities all around you.

Joni Eareckson Tada

The impossible is exactly what God does.

Oswald Chambers

Miracles broke the physical laws of the universe; forgiveness broke the moral rules.

Philip Yancey

> *But He said, "The things which are impossible*
> *with men are possible with God."*
> Luke 18:27 NKJV

∽ PRAYER

Dear God, nothing is impossible for You. Your infinite power is beyond human understanding—keep me always mindful of Your strength. When I lose hope, give me faith; when others lose hope, let me tell them of Your glory and Your works. Today, Lord, let me expect the miraculous, and let me trust in You. Amen

∽ MORE VERSES TO CONSIDER

1 Corinthians 2:9
Luke 1:37
Hebrews 2:4

STRENGTH FOR THE JOURNEY

*Those who hope in the L*ORD *will renew their strength.*
They will soar on wings like eagles; they will run
and not grow weary, they will walk and not be faint.
Isaiah 40:31 NIV

All of us must endure difficult days when our trust is tested and our strength is sapped. Thankfully, even on the darkest days, we need not endure our troubles alone. God's Word promises that He will renew our strength when we offer our hearts and prayers to Him.

Have you "tapped in" to the power of God, or are you muddling along under your own power? If you are weary, worried, fretful, or fearful, then it is time to turn to a strength much greater than your own.

The Bible tells us that we can do all things through the power of our risen Savior, Jesus Christ. Our challenge, then, is clear: we must place Christ where He belongs: at the very center of our lives. When we do so, we will surely discover that He offers us the strength to live victoriously in this world and eternally in the next.

When God is our strength, it is strength indeed; when our strength is our own, it is only weakness.

St. Augustine

Prayer plumes the wings of God's young eaglets so that they may learn to mount above the clouds. Prayer brings inner strength to God's warriors and sends them forth to spiritual battle with their muscles firm and their armor in place.

C. H. Spurgeon

God is the One who provides our strength, not only to cope with the demands of the day but also to rise above them. May we look to Him for the strength to soar.

Jim Gallery

Jesus is not a strong man making men and women who gather around Him weak. He is the Strong creating the strong.

E. Stanley Jones

I can do all things through Christ who strengthens me.
Philippians 4:13 NKJV

PRAYER

Dear Lord, let me turn to You for strength. When I am weak, You lift me up. When my spirit is crushed, You comfort me. When I am victorious, Your Word reminds me to be humble. Today and every day, I will turn to You, Father, for strength, for hope, for wisdom, and for salvation. Amen

MORE VERSES TO CONSIDER

2 Corinthians 12:9
Exodus 15:2
Philippians 4:13
Psalm 46:1

THE COURAGE
TO DREAM

Is anything too hard for the LORD?
Genesis 18:14 KJV

Are you willing to entertain the possibility that God has big plans in store for you? Hopefully so. Yet sometimes, especially if you've recently experienced a life-altering disappointment, you may find it difficult to envision a brighter future for yourself and your family. If so, it's time to reconsider your own capabilities . . . and God's.

Your heavenly Father created you with unique gifts and untapped talents; your job is to tap them. When you do, you'll begin to feel an increasing sense of confidence in yourself and in your future.

It takes courage to dream big dreams. You will discover that courage when you do three things: accept the past, trust God to handle the future, and make the most of the time He has given you today.

Nothing is too difficult for God, and no dreams are too big for Him—not even yours. So start living—and dreaming—accordingly.

You cannot out-dream God.

John Eldredge

God is the only one who can make the valley of trouble a door of hope.

Catherine Marshall

No other religion, no other philosophy promises new bodies, hearts, and minds. Only in the Gospel of Christ do hurting people find such incredible hope.

Joni Eareckson Tada

The essence of optimism is that it takes no account of the present, but it is a source of inspiration, of vitality, and of hope. Where others have resigned, it enables a man to hold his head high, to claim the future for himself, and not abandon it to his enemy.

Dietrich Bonhoeffer

May he give you the desire of your heart
and make all your plans succeed.
Psalm 20:4 NIV

∽ PRAYER

Dear Lord, give me the courage to dream and the faithfulness to trust in Your perfect plan. When I am worried or weary, give me strength for today and hope for tomorrow. Keep me mindful of Your healing power, Your infinite love, and Your eternal salvation. Amen

∽ MORE VERSES TO CONSIDER

Proverbs 29:18
Hebrews 11:1
Proverbs 24:14
Romans 15:3

THE POWER OF OUR THOUGHTS

*Finally brothers, whatever is true, whatever is honorable,
whatever is just, whatever is pure, whatever is lovely,
whatever is commendable—if there is any moral excellence
and if there is any praise—dwell on these things.*

Philippians 4:8 HCSB

Thoughts are intensely powerful things. Our thoughts have the power to lift us up or drag us down; they have the power to energize us or deplete us, to inspire us to greater accomplishments or to make those accomplishments impossible.

Bishop Fulton Sheen correctly observed, "The mind is like a clock that is constantly running down. It needs to be wound up daily with good thoughts." But sometimes, even for the most faithful believers, winding up our intellectual clocks is difficult indeed.

If negative thoughts have left you worried, exhausted, or both, it's time to readjust your thought patterns. Negative thinking is habit-forming; thankfully, so is positive thinking. And it's up to you to train your mind to focus on God's power and your possibilities. Both are far greater than you can imagine.

We never get anywhere—nor do our conditions and circumstances change—when we look at the dark side of life.

Mrs. Charles E. Cowman

To lose heart is to lose everything.

John Eldredge

The things we think are the things that feed our souls. If we think on pure and lovely things, we shall grow pure and lovely like them; and the converse is equally true.

Hannah Whitall Smith

God is great; God is good; God loves you, and He sent His Son to die for your sins. When you keep these things in mind, you'll discover that it's hard to stay worried for long.

Marie T. Freeman

Set your mind on things above, not on things on the earth.
Colossians 3:2 NKJV

∽ PRAYER

Dear Lord, keep my thoughts focused on Your love, Your power, Your promises, and Your Son. When I am worried, I will turn to You for comfort; when I am weak, I will turn to You for strength; when I am troubled, I will turn to You for patience and perspective. Help me guard my thoughts, Father, so that I may honor You today and every day that I live. Amen

∽ MORE VERSES TO CONSIDER

1 Peter 1:13
Psalm 19:14
Romans 12:2
Proverbs 16:3

WHEN DEPRESSION STRIKES HOME

I have heard your prayer, I have seen your tears;
surely I will heal you.
2 Kings 20:5 NKJV

The sadness that accompanies any significant loss is an inevitable fact of life. In time, sadness runs its course and gradually abates. Depression, on the other hand, is a physical and emotional condition that is, in almost all cases, treatable with medication and counseling. Depression is not a disease to be taken lightly. Left untreated, it presents real dangers to patients' physical health and to their emotional well-being.

If you find yourself feeling "blue," perhaps it's a logical reaction to the ups and downs of daily life. But if your feelings of sadness have gone on longer than you think they should—or if someone close to you fears that your sadness may have evolved into clinical depression— it's time to seek professional help.

Some days are light and happy, and some days are not. When we face the inevitable dark days of life, we must choose how we will respond. Will we allow ourselves to sink even more deeply into our own sadness, or will we do the difficult work of pulling ourselves out? We bring light to the dark days of life by turning first to God, and then to trusted family members, friends, and medical professionals. When we do, the clouds will eventually part, and the sun will shine once more upon our souls.

Our vision is so limited we can hardly imagine a love that does not show itself in protection from suffering. The love of God did not protect His own Son. He will not necessarily protect us—not from anything it takes to make us like His Son. A lot of hammering and chiseling and purifying by fire will have to go into the process.

Elisabeth Elliot

In heaven, we will see that nothing, absolutely nothing, was wasted, and that every tear counted and every cry was heard.

Joni Eareckson Tada

You learn your theology most where your sorrows take you.

Martin Luther

Even in the winter, even in the midst of the storm, the sun is still there. Somewhere, up above the clouds, it still shines and warms and pulls at the life buried deep inside the brown branches and frozen earth. The sun is there! Spring will come.

Gloria Gaither

For thou wilt light my candle: the LORD my God
will enlighten my darkness.
Psalm 18:28 KJV

∽ PRAYER

Lord, sometimes our hearts are broken, but even then You never leave us. On sad days, I will turn my thoughts and my prayers to You, and in Your own time and according to Your perfect plan, You will heal my broken heart. Amen

∽ MORE VERSES TO CONSIDER

Proverbs 17:22
Proverbs 12:25
Isaiah 55:8, 12
Romans 15:13

STRENGTH FOR DIFFICULT DAYS

God is our refuge and strength,
a very present help in trouble.
Psalm 46:1 NKJV

All of us face those occasional days when the traffic jams and the dog gobbles the homework. But, when we find ourselves overtaken by the minor frustrations of life, we must catch ourselves, take a deep breath, and lift our thoughts upward. Although we are here on earth struggling to rise above the distractions of the day, we need never struggle alone. God is here—eternally and faithfully, with infinite patience and love—and, if we reach out to Him, He will restore perspective and peace to our souls.

Sometimes even the most devout Christians can become discouraged, and you are no exception. After all, you live in a world where expectations can be high and demands can be even higher.

If you find yourself enduring difficult circumstances, remember that God remains in His heaven. If you become discouraged with the direction of your day or your life, lift your thoughts and prayers to Him. He is a God of possibility not negativity. He will guide you *through* your difficulties and *beyond* them. Then, you can thank the Giver of all things good for blessings that are simply too numerous to count.

We are never stronger than the moment we admit we are weak.

Beth Moore

Notice what Jesus had to say concerning those who have wearied themselves by trying to do things in their own strength: "Come to me, all you who labor and are heavy laden, and I will give you rest."

Henry Blackaby and Claude King

God conquers only what we yield to Him. Yet, when He does, and when our surrender is complete, He fills us with a new strength that we could never have known by ourselves. His conquest is our victory!

Shirley Dobson

Be of good courage, and He shall strengthen your heart,
all you who hope in the LORD.
Psalm 31:24 NKJV

∽ PRAYER

Lord, on difficult days, I will turn to You for my strength. When my heart is heavy, I will put my trust in You. In times of frustration, I will find peace in You. And every day, whether I am happy or sad, I will praise You for Your glorious works and for the gift of Your Son. Amen

∽ MORE VERSES TO CONSIDER

Isaiah 40:28-31
Matthew 11:28-30
Philippians 4:13
Psalm 105:4-5

11

ASKING GOD

Ask, and it will be given to you; seek, and you will find; knock, and it will be opened to you. For everyone who asks receives, and he who seeks finds, and to him who knocks it will be opened.

Matthew 7:7-8 NKJV

Have you fervently asked God to restore your hope for tomorrow? Have you asked Him for guidance and strength? If so, then you're continually inviting your Creator to reveal Himself in a variety of ways. As a follower of Christ, you must do no less.

Jesus made it clear to His disciples: they should petition God to meet their needs. So should we. Genuine, heartfelt prayer produces powerful changes in us *and* in our world. When we lift our hearts to God, we open ourselves to a never-ending source of divine wisdom and infinite love.

Do you have questions about your future that you simply can't answer? Do you have needs that you simply can't meet by yourself? Do you sincerely seek to know God's purpose for your life? If so, ask Him for direction, for protection, and for strength—and then keep asking Him every day that you live. Whatever your need, no matter how great or small, pray about it and never lose hope. God is not just near; He is here, and He's perfectly capable of answering your prayers. Now, it's up to you to ask.

We honor God by asking for great things when they are a part of His promise. We dishonor Him and cheat ourselves when we ask for molehills where He has promised mountains.

Vance Havner

God's help is always available, but it is only given to those who seek it.

Max Lucado

God will help us become the people we are meant to be, if only we will ask Him.

Hannah Whitall Smith

God makes prayer as easy as possible for us. He's completely approachable and available, and He'll never mock or upbraid us for bringing our needs before Him.

Shirley Dobson

You do not have, because you do not ask God.
James 4:2 NIV

✆ PRAYER

Dear Lord, today I will ask You for the things I need. In every circumstance, in every season of life, I will come to you in prayer. You know the desires of my heart, Lord; grant them, I ask. Yet not my will, Father, but Your will be done. Amen

✆ MORE VERSES TO CONSIDER

John 16:23-24 *The best*
Philippians 4:6
John 15:16
John 14:12-14

12

WHEN CHANGE IS DIFFICULT

There is a time for everything,
and a season for every activity under heaven.
Ecclesiastes 3:1 NIV

Our world is in a state of constant change. God is not. At times, the world seems to be trembling beneath our feet. But we can be comforted in the knowledge that our heavenly Father is the rock that cannot be shaken. His Word promises, "I am the LORD, I do not change" (Malachi 3:6 NKJV).

Every day that we live, we mortals encounter a multitude of changes—some good, some not so good. And on occasion, all of us must endure life-changing personal losses that leave us breathless. When we do, our loving heavenly Father stands ready to protect us, to comfort us, to guide us, and, in time, to heal us.

Are you anxious about situations that you cannot control? Take your anxieties to God. Are you troubled? Take your troubles to Him. Does your corner of the world seem to be trembling beneath your feet? Seek protection from the One who cannot be moved. The same God who created the universe will protect you if you ask Him . . . so ask Him . . . and then serve Him with willing hands and a trusting heart. Then, you can be comforted: It is precisely because your Savior *does not change* that you can face *your* challenges with courage for today and hope for tomorrow.

More often than not, when something looks like it's the absolute end, it is really the beginning.

Charles Swindoll

We are either the masters or the victims of our attitudes. It is a matter of personal choice. Who we are today is the result of choices we made yesterday. Tomorrow, we will become what we choose today. To change means to choose to change.

John Maxwell

God doesn't always change the circumstances, but He can change us to meet the circumstances. That's what it means to live by faith.

Warren Wiersbe

When all else is gone, God is still left. Nothing changes Him.

Hannah Whitall Smith

The prudent see danger and take refuge, but the simple keep going and suffer from it.

Proverbs 27:12 NIV

∽ PRAYER

Dear Lord, our world changes, but You are unchanging. When I face challenges that leave me discouraged or fearful, I will turn to You for strength and assurance. Let my trust in You—like Your love for me—be unchanging and everlasting. Amen

∽ MORE VERSES TO CONSIDER

Malachi 3:6
James 1:17
Matthew 18:3-4

BELIEF AND WORSHIP

Lord, I believe; help thou mine unbelief.

Mark 9:24 KJV

The first element of a successful life is faith: faith in God, faith in His Son, and faith in His promises. If we place our lives in God's hands, our faith is rewarded in ways that we—as human beings with clouded vision and limited understanding—can scarcely comprehend. But, if we seek to rely solely upon our own resources, or if we seek earthly success outside the boundaries of God's commandments, we reap a bitter harvest for ourselves and for our loved ones.

Do you desire the abundance and success that God has promised? Then trust Him today and every day that you live. Trust Him with every aspect of your life. Trust His promises, and trust in the saving grace of His only begotten Son. Then, when you have entrusted your future to the Giver of all things good, rest assured that your future is secure, not only for today but also for all eternity.

Faith sees the invisible, believes the unbelievable, and receives the impossible.

Corrie ten Boom

I believe in Christianity as I believe that the Sun has risen: not only because I see it, but because by it I see everything else.

C. S. Lewis

To believe God is to worship God.

Martin Luther

Understanding is the reward of faith. Therefore, seek not to understand that you may believe, but believe that you may understand.

St. Augustine

Jesus turned and saw her. "Take heart, daughter," he said, "your faith has healed you." And the woman was healed from that moment.
Matthew 9:22 NIV

∞ PRAYER

Lord, when I trust in the things of this earth, I will be disappointed. But, when I put my faith in You, I am secure. In every aspect of my life, Father, let me place my hope and my trust in Your infinite wisdom and Your boundless grace. Amen

∞ MORE VERSES TO CONSIDER

John 20:27
Mark 9:23
John 14:12-14
1 John 5:13

14

CHOOSING
ONE'S
ATTITUDE

A merry heart does good, like medicine.

Proverbs 17:22 NKJV

The Christian life is a cause for celebration, but sometimes we don't feel much like celebrating. In fact, when the weight of the world seems to bear down upon our shoulders, celebration may be the last thing on our minds . . . but it shouldn't be. As God's children, we are all blessed beyond measure on good days *and* bad. *This* day is a nonrenewable resource—once it's gone, it's gone forever. We should give thanks for this day while using it for the glory of God.

What will be your attitude today? Will you be fearful, angry, bored, or worried? Will you be cynical, bitter, or pessimistic? If so, God wants to have a little talk with you.

God created you in His own image, and He wants you to experience joy and abundance. But, God will not force His joy upon you; you must claim it for yourself. So today, and every day thereafter, celebrate the life that God has given you. Think optimistically about yourself and your future. Give thanks to the One who has given you everything, and trust in your heart that He wants to give you so much more.

Attitude is all-important. Let the soul take a quiet attitude of faith and love toward God, and from there on, the responsibility is God's. He will make good on His commitments.

A. W. Tozer

I may not be able to change the world I see around me, but I can change the way I see the world within me.

John Maxwell

Attitude is more important than the past, than education, than money, than circumstances, than what people do or say. It is more important than appearance, giftedness, or skill.

Charles Swindoll

Your attitude, not your aptitude, will determine your altitude.

Zig Ziglar

The cheerful heart has a continual feast.
Proverbs 15:15 NIV

⚮ PRAYER

Lord, I pray for an attitude that is Christlike. Whatever my circumstances, whether good or bad, triumphal or tragic, let my response reflect a God-honoring attitude of optimism, faith, and love for You. Amen

⚮ MORE VERSES TO CONSIDER

1 Peter 4:1-2
Hebrews 4:12
Philippians 2:5-8
Proverbs 4:25

FOLLOWING IN THE FOOTSTEPS

*And he said to them all, If any man will come after me, let
him deny himself, and take up his cross daily, and follow me.
For whosoever will save his life shall lose it: but whosoever
will lose his life for my sake, the same shall save it.*
                                                    Luke 9:23-24 KJV

Life is a series of decisions and choices. Each day, we make countless decisions that can bring us closer to God . . . or not. When we live according to God's commandments, we reap bountiful rewards: abundance, hope, and peace, for starters. But, when we turn our backs upon God by disobeying Him, we bring needless suffering upon ourselves *and* our families.

Do you seek to walk in the footsteps of the One from Galilee, or will you choose another path? If you sincerely seek God's peace and His blessings, then you must strive to imitate God's Son.

Thomas Brooks spoke for believers of every generation when he observed, "Christ is the sun, and all the watches of our lives should be set by the dial of his motion." Christ, indeed, is the ultimate Savior of mankind and the personal Savior of those who believe in Him. As His servants, we should walk in His footsteps as we share His love and His message with a world that needs both.

The heaviest end of the cross lies ever on His shoulders. If He bids us carry a burden, He carries it also.

C. H. Spurgeon

Begin to know Him now, and finish never.

Oswald Chambers

A believer comes to Christ; a disciple follows after Him.

Vance Havner

You cannot cooperate with Jesus in becoming what He wants you to become and simultaneously be what the world desires to make you. If you would say, "Take the world but give me Jesus," then you must deny yourself and take up your cross. The simple truth is that your "self" must be put to death in order for you to get to the point where for you to live is Christ. What will it be? The world and you, or Jesus and you? You do have a choice to make.

Kay Arthur

*But whoever keeps His word, truly the love of God is
perfected in him. By this we know that we are in Him.
He who says he abides in Him ought himself
also to walk just as He walked.*

1 John 2:5-6 NKJV

☽ PRAYER

Dear Lord, You sent Your Son so that I might have
abundant life *and* eternal life. Thank You, Father, for my
Savior, Christ Jesus. I will follow Him, honor Him, and
share His good news, this day and every day. Amen

☽ MORE VERSES TO CONSIDER

John 12:26
Matthew 6:24
Matthew 10:38-39
John 21:19

HOPE FOR TOMORROW, JOY FOR TODAY

This is the day the LORD has made;
let us rejoice and be glad in it.
Psalm 118:24 NIV

This day is a blessed gift from God. And as Christians, we have countless reasons to rejoice. Yet on some days, when the demands of life threaten to overwhelm us, we may lose sight of our blessings. Instead of celebrating God's glorious creation, we may find ourselves frustrated by the obligations of today and worried by the uncertainties of tomorrow.

Every day should be a time for prayer and celebration as we consider the good news of our salvation through Jesus Christ. May we—as believers who have so much to celebrate—never fail to praise our Creator by rejoicing in His glorious handiwork.

The familiar words of Psalm 118:24 remind us that "This is the day the LORD has made." Whatever this day holds for you, begin it and end it with God as your partner and Christ as your Savior. And throughout the day, give thanks to the One who created you and saved you. God's love for you is infinite. Accept it with praise on your lips and hope in your heart . . . and be thankful.

Christ and joy go together.

E. Stanley Jones

Gratitude changes the pangs of memory into a tranquil joy.

Dietrich Bonhoeffer

There is not one blade of grass, there is no color in this world that is not intended to make us rejoice.

John Calvin

If you're a thinking Christian, you will be a joyful Christian.

Marie T. Freeman

*Now may the God of hope fill you with all joy and peace
in believing, that you may abound in hope by
the power of the Holy Spirit.*

Romans 15:13 NKJV

∞ PRAYER

Lord, You have given me another day of life; let me celebrate this day, and let me use it according to Your plan. I praise You, Father, for my life and for the friends and family members who make it rich. Enable me to live each moment to the fullest as I give thanks for Your creation, for Your love, and for Your Son. Amen

∞ MORE VERSES TO CONSIDER

Philippians 4:4
1 Chronicles 16:10-11
John 10:10
John 17:13

ENTRUSTING TOMORROW TO GOD

But if we hope for what we do not yet have,
we wait for it patiently.
Romans 8:25 NIV

Sometimes the future seems bright, and sometimes it does not. Yet even when *we* cannot see the possibilities of tomorrow, God can. As believers, our challenge is to trust an uncertain future to an all-powerful God.

When we trust God, we should trust Him without reservation. We should steel ourselves against the inevitable disappointments of the day, secure in the knowledge that our heavenly Father has a plan for the future that only He can see.

Can you place your future into the hands of a loving and all-knowing God? Can you live amid the uncertainties of today, knowing that God has dominion over all your tomorrows? If you can, you are wise and you are blessed. When you trust God with everything you are and everything you have, He will bless you now *and* forever.

Every experience God gives us, every person He brings into our lives, is the perfect preparation for the future that only He can see.

Corrie ten Boom

Do not limit the limitless God! With Him, face the future unafraid because you are never alone.

Mrs. Charles E. Cowman

That we may not complain of what is, let us see God's hand in all events; and, that we may not be afraid of what shall be, let us see all events in God's hand.

Matthew Henry

There is no greater joy than the peace and assurance of knowing that, whatever the future may hold, you are secure in the loving arms of the Savior.

Billy Graham

For I know the thoughts that I think toward you,
*says the L*ORD*, thoughts of peace and not of evil, to give you*
a future and a hope. Then you will call upon Me and
go and pray to Me, and I will listen to you.
Jeremiah 29:11-12 NKJV

∽ PRAYER

Dear Lord, I will turn my concerns over to You. I will trust Your love, Your wisdom, Your plan, Your promises, and Your Son—today and every day that I live. Amen

∽ MORE VERSES TO CONSIDER

Proverbs 14:24
Proverbs 27:1
Proverbs 31:25-27

18

MAKING ALL THINGS NEW

Then He who sat on the throne said,
"Behold, I make all things new."
Revelation 21:5 NKJV

God has the power to transform your life *if* you invite Him to do so. Your decision is straightforward: whether or not to allow the Father's transforming power to work in you and through you. God stands at the door and waits; all you must do is knock. When you do, God always answers.

Sometimes, the demands of daily life may drain you of strength or rob you of the joy that is rightfully yours in Christ. But even on your darkest day, you may be comforted by the knowledge that God has the power to renew your spirit and your life.

Are you in need of a new beginning? If so, turn your heart toward God in prayer. Are you weak or worried? Take the time—or, more accurately, *make* the time—to delve deeply into God's Holy Word. Are you spiritually depleted? Call upon fellow believers to support you, and call upon Christ to renew your sense of joy and thanksgiving. When you do, you'll discover that the Creator of the universe is in the business of making all things new—including you.

No matter how badly we have failed, we can always get up and begin again. Our God is the God of new beginnings.

Warren Wiersbe

The amazing thing about Jesus is that He doesn't just patch up our lives, He gives us a brand new sheet, a clean slate to start over, all new.

Gloria Gaither

God is not running an antique shop! He is making all things new!

Vance Havner

I wish I could make it all new again; I can't. But God can. "He restores my soul," wrote the shepherd. God doesn't reform; He restores. He doesn't camouflage the old; He restores the new. The Master Builder will pull out the original plan and restore it. He will restore the vigor; He will restore the energy. He will restore the hope. He will restore the soul.

Max Lucado

Therefore if anyone is in Christ, he is a new creature;
the old things passed away; behold, new things have come.
2 Corinthians 5:17 HCSB

∞ PRAYER

Dear Lord, You have the power to make all things new. When I grow weary, let me turn my thoughts and my prayers to You. When I am discouraged, restore my faith in You. Renew my strength, Father, and let me draw comfort and courage from Your promises and from Your unending love. Amen

∞ MORE VERSES TO CONSIDER

Romans 12:2
Psalm 23:2-3
Psalm 51:10
Psalm 147:3

LIVING COURAGEOUSLY DAY BY DAY

*Therefore we do not give up; even though our outer person
is being destroyed, our inner person is being
renewed day by day.*
2 Corinthians 4:16 HCSB

Every human life is a tapestry of events: some grand, some not so grand, and some down-right tragic. When we reach the mountaintops of life, praising God is easy. In the moment of triumph, we trust God's plan. But, when the storm clouds form overhead and we find ourselves in the dark valley of despair, our faith is stretched, sometimes to the breaking point. As Christians, we can be comforted: Wherever we find ourselves, whether at the top of the mountain or the depths of the valley, God is there, and because He cares for us, we can live courageously.

Believing Christians have every reason to be courageous. After all, the ultimate battle has already been fought and won on the cross at Calvary. But, even dedicated followers of Christ may find their courage tested by the inevitable disappointments and tragedies that occur in the lives of believers and nonbelievers alike.

The next time you find your courage tested to the limit, remember that God is as near as your next breath, and remember that He offers salvation to His children. He is your shield and your strength; He is your protector and your deliverer. Call upon Him in your hour of need and then be comforted: He is not simply near; He is here.

What is courage? It is the ability to be strong in trust, in conviction, in obedience. To be courageous is to step out in faith—to trust and obey, no matter what.

Kay Arthur

Daniel looked into the face of God and would not fear the face of a lion.

C. H. Spurgeon

To fear and not be afraid, that is the paradox of faith.

A. W. Tozer

Down through the centuries, in times of trouble and trial, God has brought courage to the hearts of those who love Him. The Bible is filled with assurances of God's help and comfort in every kind of trouble which might cause fears to arise in the human heart. You can look ahead with promise, hope, and joy.

Billy Graham

This hope we have as an anchor of the soul,
a hope both sure and steadfast.
Hebrews 6:19 NASB

∞ PRAYER

Lord, let me turn to You for courage and for strength. When I am fearful, keep me mindful of Your promises. When I am anxious, let me turn my thoughts and prayers to the priceless gift of Your Son. You are with me always, heavenly Father, and I will face the challenges of this day with trust and assurance in You. Amen

∞ MORE VERSES TO CONSIDER

Joshua 1:9
Proverbs 29:25
Psalm 27:1
Psalm 71:1

HOPE IS CONTAGIOUS

*So then we pursue the things which make for peace
and the building up of one another.*

Romans 14:19 NASB

Hope, like other human emotions, is contagious. If you associate with hope-filled, enthusiastic people, their enthusiasm will have a tendency to lift your spirits. But if you find yourself spending too much time in the company of naysayers, pessimists, or cynics, your thoughts, like theirs, will tend to be negative.

Are you a hopeful, optimistic Christian? And do you associate with like-minded people? If so, then you're availing yourself of a priceless gift: the encouragement of fellow believers. But, if you find yourself focusing on the negative aspects of life, perhaps it is time to search out a few new friends.

As a faithful follower of the man from Galilee, you have every reason to be hopeful. So today, look for reasons to celebrate God's endless blessings. And while you're at it, look for people who will join with you in the celebration. You'll be better for their company, and they'll be better for yours.

Make the least of all that goes and the most of all that comes. Don't regret what is past. Cherish what you have. Look forward to all that is to come. And most important of all, rely moment by moment on Jesus Christ.

Gigi Graham Tchividjian

The people whom I have seen succeed best in life have always been cheerful and hopeful people who went about their business with a smile on their faces.

Charles Kingsley

If our hearts have been attuned to God through an abiding faith in Christ, the result will be joyous optimism and good cheer.

Billy Graham

A positive attitude will have positive results because attitudes are contagious.

Zig Ziglar

A wise man will hear and increase in learning,
and a man of understanding will acquire wise counsel.

Proverbs 1:5 NASB

∞ PRAYER

Dear Lord, make me a source of genuine, lasting encouragement to my family and friends. Today, I will celebrate Your blessings, and I will share Your good news with those who cross my path. Let my words and deeds be worthy of Your Son, the One who gives me strength and salvation. Amen

∞ MORE VERSES TO CONSIDER

Psalm 23:5-6
Psalm 31:24
Psalm 51:8

21

MOUNTAIN-MOVING FAITH

If you have faith as a mustard seed, you will say to this mountain, "Move from here to there," and it will move; and nothing will be impossible for you.

Matthew 17:20 NKJV

Jesus taught His disciples that if they had faith, they could move mountains. You can too. When you place your faith, your trust, indeed your life in the hands of Christ Jesus, you'll be amazed at the marvelous things He can do. So strengthen your faith through praise, through worship, through Bible study, and through prayer. And trust God's plans. With Him, all things are possible, and He stands ready to open a world of possibilities to you . . . *if* you have faith.

Concentration camp survivor Corrie ten Boom relied on faith during her long months of imprisonment and torture. Later, despite the fact that four of her family members had died in Nazi death camps, Corrie's faith was unshaken. She wrote, "There is no pit so deep that God's love is not deeper still." Christians take note: genuine faith in God means faith in all circumstances, happy or sad, joyful or tragic.

If your faith is being tested to the point of breaking, remember that Your Savior is near. If you reach out to Him in faith, He will give you peace and heal your broken spirit. Reach out today. If you touch even the smallest fragment of the Master's garment, He will make you whole.

Faith expects from God what is beyond all expectation.

Andrew Murray

The Christian life is one of faith, where we find ourselves routinely overdriving our headlights but knowing it's okay because God is in control and has a purpose behind it.

Bill Hybels

True faith is never found alone; it is accompanied by expectation.

C. S. Lewis

Faith in small things has repercussions that ripple all the way out. In a huge, dark room a little match can light up the place.

Joni Eareckson Tada

*Cast your burden upon the LORD and He will sustain you:
He will never allow the righteous to be shaken.*
Psalm 55:22 NASB

∽ PRAYER

Lord, when this world becomes a fearful place, give me faith. When I am filled with uncertainty and doubt, give me faith. In the dark moments, help me to remember that You are always near and that You can overcome any challenge. And, in the joyous moments, keep me mindful that every gift comes from You. In every aspect of my life, Lord, and in every circumstance, give me faith. Amen

∽ MORE VERSES TO CONSIDER

Philippians 4:13
Mark 9:23
Mark 5:37
Luke 11:9-13

22

HOPE AT THE FOOT OF THE CROSS

Your attitude should be the same as that of Christ Jesus: Who, being in very nature God, did not consider equality with God something to be grasped, but made himself nothing, taking the very nature of a servant, being made in human likeness. And being found in appearance as a man, he humbled himself and became obedient to death— even death on a cross!

Philippians 2:5-8 NIV

Jesus loved you so much that He endured unspeakable humiliation and suffering *for you*. How will you respond to Christ's sacrifice? Will you take up His cross and follow Him (Luke 9:23), or will you choose another path? When you place your hopes squarely at the foot of the cross, when you place Jesus squarely at the center of your life, you will be blessed.

The nineteenth-century writer Hannah Whitall Smith observed, "The crucial question for each of us is this: What do you think of Jesus, and do you yet have a personal acquaintance with Him?" Indeed, the answer to that question determines the quality, the course, and the direction of our lives today and for all eternity.

The old familiar hymn begins, "What a friend we have in Jesus . . . ." No truer words were ever penned. Jesus is the sovereign Friend and ultimate Savior of mankind. Christ showed enduring love for His believers by willingly sacrificing His own life so that we might have eternal life. Now, it is our turn to become His friend.

Let us love our Savior, praise Him, and share His message of salvation with our neighbors and with the world. When we do, we demonstrate that our acquaintance with the Master is not a passing fancy; it is, instead, the cornerstone and the touchstone of our lives.

There is no detour to holiness. Jesus came to the resurrection through the cross, not around it.

Leighton Ford

The cross is not the terrible end to an otherwise God-fearing and happy life, but it meets us at the beginning of our communion with Christ. When Christ calls a man, He bids him come and die.

Dietrich Bonhoeffer

On the eve of the cross, Jesus made His decision. He would rather go to hell for you than go to heaven without you.

Max Lucado

It costs God nothing, so far as we know, to create nice things: but to convert rebellious wills cost Him crucifixion.

C. S. Lewis

*Let not your heart be troubled; you believe in God,
believe also in Me.*
John 14:1 NKJV

∞ PRAYER

Dear Jesus, You are my Savior and my protector. Give me the courage to trust You completely. Today, I will praise You, I will honor You, and I will live according to Your commandments, so that through me, others might come to know Your perfect love. Amen

∞ MORE VERSES TO CONSIDER

Job 19:25
Luke 24:6
1 Peter 1:3
John 16:22

23

PEACE THAT PASSES UNDERSTANDING

*And the peace of God, which transcends all understanding,
will guard your hearts and your minds in Christ Jesus.*

Philippians 4:7 NIV

Through His Son, God offers a "peace that passes all understanding," but He does not force His peace upon us. God's peace is a blessing that we, as children of a loving Father, must claim for ourselves . . . but sometimes we are slow to do so. Why? Because we are fallible human beings with limited understanding and limited faith.

Have you found the lasting peace that can be yours through Jesus, or are you still rushing after the illusion of "peace and happiness" that the world promises but cannot deliver?

Today, as a gift to yourself, to your family, and to your friends, claim the inner peace that is your spiritual birthright: the peace of Jesus Christ. It is offered freely; it has been paid for in full; it is yours for the asking. So ask. And then share.

Thou hast formed us for Thyself, and our hearts are restless till they find rest in Thee.

St. Augustine

The peace that Jesus gives is never engineered by circumstances on the outside.

Oswald Chambers

A great many people are trying to make peace, but that has already been done. God has not left it for us to do; all we have to do is to enter into it.

D. L. Moody

Peace does not mean to be in a place where there is no noise, trouble, or hard work. Peace means to be in the midst of all those things and still be calm in your heart.

Catherine Marshall

*Come to me, all you who are weary and burdened, and I will
give you rest. Take my yoke upon you and learn from me,
for I am gentle and humble in heart, and you will find rest
for your souls. For my yoke is easy and my burden is light.*
Matthew 11:28-30 NIV

∞ PRAYER

Dear Lord, the peace that the world offers is fleeting, but
You offer a peace that is perfect and eternal. Let me take
my concerns and burdens to You, Father, and let me feel
the spiritual abundance that You offer through the person
of Your Son, the Prince of Peace. Amen

∞ MORE VERSES TO CONSIDER

Psalm 119:165
Philippians 1:2
John 14:27
Isaiah 26:3

FOCUSING ON THE FATHER

Be still, and know that I am God . . . .

Psalm 46:10 KJV

Are you so busy that you rush through the day with scarcely a single moment for quiet contemplation and prayer? If so, it's time to reorder your priorities.

We live in a noisy world, a world filled with distractions, frustrations, and complications. But if we allow the distractions of a clamorous world to separate us from God's peace, we do ourselves a profound disservice. If we are to maintain righteous and hope-filled minds, we must take time each day for prayer and meditation. We must make ourselves still in the presence of our Creator. We must quiet our minds and our hearts so that we might sense God's will, God's love, and God's Son.

Has the busy pace of life robbed you of the peace and hope that might otherwise be yours through Jesus Christ? Nothing is more important than the time you spend with your Savior. So be still and claim that inner peace. Today.

Christian discipleship is a process of paying more and more attention to God's righteousness and less and less attention to our own; finding the meaning of our lives not by probing our moods and motives and morals, but by believing in God's will and purposes; making a map of the faithfulness of God, not charting the rise and fall of our enthusiasms.

Eugene Peterson

As long as Jesus is one of many options, He is no option.

Max Lucado

Only the man who follows the command of Jesus single-mindedly and unresistingly lets his yoke rest upon Him, finds his burden easy, and under its gentle pressure receives the power to persevere in the right way.

Dietrich Bonhoeffer

Whatever we focus on determines what we become.

E. Stanley Jones

*But seek first the kingdom of God and His righteousness,
and all these things shall be added to you.*

Matthew 6:33 NKJV

∽ PRAYER

Dear Lord, let me be still before You. When I am hurried
or distracted, slow me down and redirect my thoughts.
When I am confused, give me perspective. Keep me
mindful, Father, that You are always with me. And let me
sense Your presence today, tomorrow, and forever. Amen

∽ MORE VERSES TO CONSIDER

Hebrews 12:2
Philippians 3:15-16
Philippians 4:8-9

TRUSTING GOD'S PLAN

Do not conform any longer to the pattern of this world, but be transformed by the renewing of your mind. Then you will be able to test and approve what God's will is—his good, pleasing and perfect will.

Romans 12:2 NIV

God has plans for your life, but He won't force those plans upon you. To the contrary, He has given you free will, the ability to make decisions on your own. With that freedom to choose comes the responsibility of living with the consequences of the choices you make.

If you seek to live in accordance with God's will for your life—and you should—then you will live in accordance with His commandments. You will study God's Word, and you will be watchful for His signs. You will associate with fellow Christians who will encourage your spiritual growth, and you will listen to that inner voice that speaks to you in the quiet moments of your daily devotionals.

God intends to use you in wonderful, unexpected ways if you let Him. The decision to seek God's plan and to follow it is yours and yours alone. The consequences of that decision have implications that are both profound and eternal, so choose carefully.

Let's never forget that some of God's greatest mercies are His refusals. He says no in order that He may, in some way we cannot imagine, say yes. All His ways with us are merciful. His meaning is always love.

Elisabeth Elliot

God will not permit any troubles to come upon us unless He has a specific plan by which great blessing can come out of the difficulty.

Peter Marshall

God does not furnish us with a detailed road map. When we are with Him, we may not always know whither, but we know with whom.

Vance Havner

We are uncertain of the next step, but we are certain of God.

Oswald Chambers

Blessed is he that trusts in the LORD.
Proverbs 16:20 NIV

∞ PRAYER

Dear Lord, I am Your creation, and You created me for a reason. Give me the wisdom to follow Your direction for my life's journey. Let me do Your work here on earth by seeking Your will and living it, knowing that when I trust in You, Father, I am eternally blessed. Amen

∞ MORE VERSES TO CONSIDER

Psalm 23:8
Romans 11:33-34
Psalm 37:23-24
Psalm 25:12-13

26

FACING OUR FEARS

But He said to them, "Why are you fearful,
O you of little faith?" Then He arose and rebuked
the winds and the sea, and there was a great calm.

Matthew 8:26 NKJV

All of us may find our courage tested by the inevitable disappointments and tragedies of life. After all, ours is a world filled with uncertainty, hardship, sickness, and danger. Old Man Trouble, it seems, is never too far from the front door.

When we focus upon our fears and our doubts, we may find many reasons to lie awake at night and fret about the uncertainties of the coming day. A better strategy, of course, is to focus not upon our fears but instead upon our God.

God is as near as your next breath, and He is in control. He offers salvation to all His children, including you. God is your shield and your strength; you are His forever. So don't focus your thoughts upon the fears of the day. Instead, trust God's plan and His eternal love for you. And remember: God is good, and He has the final word.

Are you fearful? First, bow your head and pray for God's strength. Then, raise your head and look Old Man Trouble squarely in the eye. Chances are, Old Man Trouble will blink.

Jim Gallery

The Bible is a Christian's guidebook, and I believe the knowledge it sheds on pain and suffering is the great antidote to fear for suffering people. Knowledge can dissolve fear as light destroys darkness.

Philip Yancey

God alone can give us songs in the night.

C. H. Spurgeon

Fear is a self-imposed prison that will keep you from becoming what God intends for you to be.

Rick Warren

In my anguish I cried to the LORD, and he answered by setting me free. The LORD is with me; I will not be afraid. What can man do to me?

Psalm 118:5-6 NIV

∽ PRAYER

Your Word reminds me, Lord, that even when I walk through the valley of the shadow of death, I need fear no evil, for You are with me, and You comfort me. Thank You, Lord, for a perfect love that casts out fear. Let me live courageously and faithfully this day and every day. Amen

∽ MORE VERSES TO CONSIDER

Psalm 56:3
Psalm 34:4
Isaiah 43:1
Mark 5:36

THE PATH

You will show me the path of life; in Your presence is fullness of joy; at Your right hand are pleasures forevermore.

Psalm 16:11 NKJV

When Jesus addressed His disciples, He warned that each one must "take up his cross and follow me." The disciples must have known exactly what the Master meant. In Jesus' day, prisoners were forced to carry their own crosses to the location where they would be put to death. Thus, Christ's message was clear: in order to follow Him, Christ's disciples must deny themselves and, instead, trust Him completely. Nothing has changed since then.

If we are to be dutiful disciples of the One from Galilee, we must trust Him and place Him at the center of our lives. Jesus never comes "next." He is always first. He shows us the path of life; we, in turn, are asked to follow Him along that path.

Do you seek to be a worthy disciple of Jesus? Then pick up His cross today and follow in His footsteps. When you do, you can walk with confidence: He will never lead you astray.

Discipleship is a daily discipline: we follow Jesus a step at a time, a day at a time.

Warren Wiersbe

There is no way to draw closer to God unless you are in the Word of God every day. It's your compass. Your guide. You can't get where you need to go without it.

Stormie Omartian

The Bible says that being a Christian is not only a great way to die, but it's also the best way to live.

Bill Hybels

There is something incredibly comforting about knowing that the Creator is in control of your life.

Lisa Whelchel

In all your ways acknowledge Him,
and He shall direct your paths.

Proverbs 3:6 NKJV

∞ PRAYER

Dear Jesus, because I am Your disciple, I will trust You, I will obey Your teachings, and I will share Your good news. You have given me life abundant and life eternal, and I will follow You today and forever. Amen

∞ MORE VERSES TO CONSIDER

Jeremiah 29:11-12
Philippians 2:13
Proverbs 21:30
Psalm 127:1

TRUST FOR THE FUTURE

Let us hold on to the confession of our hope without
wavering, for He who promised is faithful.
Hebrews 10:23 HCSB

L ife is like a garden. Every day, God gives us opportunities to plant seeds for the future. When we plant wisely and trust God completely, the harvest is bountiful.

Are you willing to place your future in the hands of a loving and all-knowing God? Do you trust in the ultimate goodness of His plan for your life? Will you face today's challenges with optimism and hope? You should. After all, God created you for a very important reason: *His* reason. And you still have important work to do: *His* work.

Today, as you live in the present and look to the future, remember that God has a plan for you. Act—and believe—accordingly.

Never be afraid to trust an unknown future to a known God.

Corrie ten Boom

Do not limit the limitless God! With Him, face the future unafraid because you are never alone.

Mrs. Charles E. Cowman

Take courage. We walk in the wilderness today and in the Promised Land tomorrow.

D. L. Moody

That we may not complain of what is, let us see God's hand in all events; and, that we may not be afraid of what shall be, let us see all events in God's hand.

Matthew Henry

The Christian believes in a fabulous future.

Billy Graham

As for God, His way is perfect; the word of the LORD is proven; He is a shield to all who trust in Him.

Psalm 18:30 NKJV

∞ PRAYER

Dear Lord, as I look to the future, I will place my trust in You. If I become discouraged, I will turn to You. If I am afraid, I will seek strength in You. You are my Father, and I will place my hope, my trust, and my faith in You. Amen

∞ MORE VERSES TO CONSIDER

Proverbs 24:14
Matthew 6:34
Romans 8:38
Hebrews 13:8

29

A GROWING FAITH

*Therefore, laying aside all malice, all deceit, hypocrisy, envy,
and all evil speaking, as newborn babes, desire the pure milk
of the word, that you may grow thereby.*

1 Peter 2:1-2 NKJV

The journey toward spiritual maturity lasts a lifetime: As Christians, we can and should continue to grow in the love and the knowledge of our Savior as long as we live. When we cease to grow, either emotionally or spiritually, we do ourselves and our loved ones a profound disservice. But, if we study God's Word, if we obey His commandments, and if we live in the center of His will, we will not be "stagnant" believers; we will, instead, be growing Christians . . . and that's exactly what God wants for our lives.

Many of life's most important lessons are painful to learn. During times of heartbreak and hardship, God stands ready to protect us. As Psalm 147:3 promises, "He heals the brokenhearted and bandages their wounds" (NCV). In His own time and according to His master plan, God will heal us if we invite Him into our hearts.

Spiritual growth need not take place only in times of adversity. We must seek to grow in our knowledge and love of the Lord every day that we live. In those quiet moments when we open our hearts to God, the One who made us keeps remaking us. He gives us direction, perspective, wisdom, and courage. The appropriate moment to accept those spiritual gifts is the present one.

When you enroll in the "school of faith," you never know what may happen next. The life of faith presents challenges that keep you going—and keep you growing!

Warren Wiersbe

Walking in faith brings you to the Word of God. There you will be healed, cleansed, fed, nurtured, equipped, and matured.

Kay Arthur

The measure of faith must always determine the measure of power and of blessing. Faith can only live by feeding on what is Divine, on God Himself.

Andrew Murray

Faith in faith is pointless. Faith in a living, active God moves mountains.

Beth Moore

A Christian is never in a state of completion but always in the process of becoming.

Martin Luther

But grow in the grace and knowledge of our Lord and Savior Jesus Christ. To Him be the glory both now and forever.

2 Peter 3:18 NKJV

∞ PRAYER

Dear Lord, when I open myself to You, I am blessed. Let me accept Your love and Your wisdom, Father. Show me Your way, and deliver me from the painful mistakes that I make when I stray from Your commandments. Let me live according to Your Word, and let me grow in my faith every day that I live. Amen

∞ MORE VERSES TO CONSIDER

Ephesians 3:18-19
2 Timothy 3:14-15
James 1:2-4
Matthew 11:29

FOR GOD SO LOVED THE WORLD

*For God so loved the world, that he gave his only begotten
Son, that whosoever believeth in him should not perish,
but have everlasting life.*

John 3:16 KJV

Make no mistake about it: God loves our world. He loves it so much, in fact, that He sent His only begotten Son to die for our sins. And now we, as believers, are challenged to return God's love by obeying His commandments and honoring His Son.

When you open your heart and accept God's love, you are transformed not just for today but for all eternity. When you accept the Father's love, you feel differently about yourself, your world, your neighbors, your family, and your church. When you feel God's presence and invite His Son into your heart, you begin to feel a tug on your heartstrings to share His message and to obey His commandments.

God loved this world so much that He sent His Son to save it. And now only one real question remains for you: what, friend, will you do in response to God's love? The answer should be obvious: if you haven't already done so, accept Jesus Christ as Your Savior. He's waiting patiently for you, but please don't make Him wait another minute longer.

God has pursued us from farther than space and longer than time.

John Eldredge

"How can I give you up, Ephraim? How can I hand you over, Israel?" Substitute your own name for Ephraim and Israel. At the heart of the gospel is a God who deliberately surrenders to the wild, irresistible power of love.

Philip Yancey

The love of God is revealed in that He laid down His life for His enemies.

Oswald Chambers

Incomprehensible and immutable is the love of God. For it was not after we were reconciled to Him by the blood of His Son that He began to love us, but He loved us before the foundation of the world, that with His only begotten Son we too might be sons of God before we were anything at all.

St. Augustine

God made man. Man rejected God. God won't give up until He wins him back.

Max Lucado

But as for me, I will hope continually,
and will praise You yet more and more.

Psalm 71:14 NASB

∞ PRAYER

Thank You, Lord, for Your love. Your love is boundless, infinite, and eternal. Today, as I pause and reflect upon Your love for me, let me share that love with all those who cross my path. And, as an expression of my love for You, Father, let me share the saving message of Your Son with a world in desperate need of His hope, His peace, and His salvation. Amen

∞ MORE VERSES TO CONSIDER

Psalm 63:1-3
John 15:9
Song of Solomon 2:4
Ephesians 1:4-5